IMAGES
of America

ACADIA
NATIONAL PARK

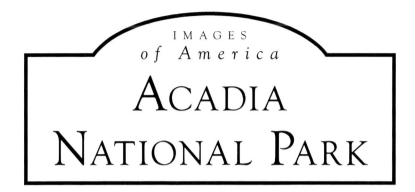

IMAGES
of America

ACADIA
NATIONAL PARK

Anne M. Kozak
with Josh Winer and Sam Putnam

ARCADIA
PUBLISHING

Copyright © 2023 by Anne M. Kozak with Josh Winer and Sam Putnam
ISBN 978-1-4671-0986-4

Published by Arcadia Publishing
Charleston, South Carolina

Printed in the United States of America

Library of Congress Control Number: 2022951069

For all general information, please contact Arcadia Publishing:
Telephone 843-853-2070
Fax 843-853-0044
E-mail sales@arcadiapublishing.com
For customer service and orders:
Toll-Free 1-888-313-2665

Visit us on the Internet at www.arcadiapublishing.com

*This book is dedicated to my grandchildren, all
of whom have brought me much joy.*

CONTENTS

ACKNOWLEDGMENTS

Special thanks go to Genie Thorndike and Barbara Carter. Genie's editing skills and perceptive comments enhanced the relevance of the text for the photographs; we appreciated her willingness to review text on short notice. For the past year, Barbara, the administrative assistant to College of the Atlantic's faculty, has prepared various iterations of the manuscript and compiled all the front matter, chapters, and bibliography. We also thank our editor, Caitrin Cunningham; acquisitions editor, Erin Vosgien; and Arcadia Publishing's production staff, including Michael Litchfield, for their support, encouragement, and professionalism.

A special thank you goes to Christiaan van Heerden and Paul MacQuinn. Christiaan shared a 1917 album of the Satterlee family. Paul not only shared images of moving the bridge over the carriage road linking Eagle Lake and Witch Hole Pond but explained the technical aspects of the project and then reviewed the text.

We thank College of the Atlantic for providing space and allowing us to use the college's resources. Lothar Holzke and Jarly Bobadilla consistently aided us in resolving technical issues. We appreciate Owen Mendelaar's willingness to scan several of the photographs. We thank Earl Brechlin, Rob Levin, Malek Hinnawi, Thomas Gonye, Ken Hill, Ashleigh Conti, Steve Ressel, and Sheridan Steele for the images they shared with us. At Friends of Acadia (FOA), Julia Walker Thomas and Stephanie Clement both made FOA's extensive photograph collection available to us. At Acadia National Park, Rebecca Cole-Will, Charlie Jacobi, and Marie Yarborough not only gave us perceptive insights but also provided us with digital images.

Dick Cough, Sue Leiter, Laura Edwards, and Helen Koch supported us throughout the project, and Helen, on short notice, photographed documents. We thank Sheldon Goldthwait for his genealogy research. A number of archivists helped us locate and use a variety of images. They include Debbie Dyer, Carolyn Rapkievan, and Mazie Smallidge from the Bar Harbor Historical Society; Isabella Connelly from the Jesup Memorial Library; Sadie Cooley from the Southwest Harbor Public Library; Daniella Accettura from the Northeast Harbor Library; Patrick Callaway from the Mount Desert Island Historical Society; and Kirk Mahoney, director and state historic preservation officer from the Maine Historic Preservation Commission. To all of the above and our families, a sincere thank you.

INTRODUCTION

Unlike parks in the West that were carved out of federal lands, Acadia was given to the nation acre by acre by many different people over time. Initially gifts of land came from wealthy summer residents who had a desire both to preserve Mount Desert Island's natural beauty and to ensure public access.

While George Bucknam Dorr is considered the "father of Acadia," others played pivotal roles. Dorr purchased lands and lobbied influential friends, both men and women, to help establish Acadia in 1916, but Acadia's roots go back to the 1880s—a time when a strong conservation ethic was developing. By 1880, the island was one of the most popular summer retreats in the United States, and those who came here to escape cities wanted to protect the island's fresh air and natural beauty.

The 1880s were also a time when people enjoyed exploring and researching natural history. Charles Eliot, son of Harvard president Charles W. Eliot and a summer resident of Northeast Harbor, persuaded some college friends to come to Mount Desert Island and explore the island's geology, flora, and fauna. They camped on Somes Sound and called themselves the Champlain Society after Samuel de Champlain, who first discovered the island in 1604.

Following his son's early death in 1897 at the age of 38, Eliot, spurred by his son's writings about land preservation and as a way of honoring his memory, invited a number of people, including Dorr, to a meeting in Seal Harbor. Dorr brought his neighbors—George Vanderbilt and John S. Kennedy, a New York banker.

As Dorr notes in *The Story of Acadia National Park*, Eliot's purpose in convening the meeting was to establish a land trust. This group established the Hancock County Trustees of Public Reservations (HCTPR) in 1901, and it was officially incorporated as a tax-free organization by the Maine Legislature in 1903. The trust's charter states its purpose: "To acquire, by devise, gift, or purchase, and to own, arrange, hold, maintain or improve for public use lands in Hancock County, Maine, which by reason of scenic beauty, historical interest, sanitary advantage or other like reasons may become available for such purpose."

Dorr became the point person for acquiring land and for maintaining contacts with local people on Mount Desert Island as well as its wealthy summer residents. Dorr was uniquely qualified for this position, as he was a well-connected Harvard graduate, had travelled extensively throughout Europe, and came from a wealthy Boston family who purchased land on Compass Harbor in 1868 and built Old Farm there in 1878—a home where Dorr, beginning in 1914, lived year-round and entertained various government officials and members of Congress. As a wealthy bachelor, Dorr could travel to Augusta, New York, or Washington on a moment's notice and could rush back to Bar Harbor to exercise a land option or secure a purchase.

Following incorporation, the trustees received two early gifts—a hilltop overlooking Jordan Pond and land on a bold cliff along Cooksey Drive in Seal Harbor. It was not until 1908 that another significant gift was received. Eliza Homans of Boston and Bar Harbor, a longtime friend of the Dorrs and Eliots, donated the Bowl and Beehive as well as other land on Champlain Mountain.

A donation from John S. Kennedy enabled the trustees to purchase 100 acres on the summit of Cadillac Mountain. In 1910, seven Seal Harbor residents bought 3,600 acres—land that included the South Bubble, Pemetic Mountain, and the western side of Cadillac. In 1912, several Northeast Harbor residents raised $7,000 to purchase Jordan and Sargent Mountains. Over time, the trustees received 129 gifts varying from an acre by a brook to large tracts of wild land—land that by 1916 totaled more than 6,000 acres.

After two local people failed to establish a spring in the area of the Great and Little Meadows, the latter now called the Tarn, Dorr inquired about the price and thought the price tag of $5,000 was too high. Since there did not seem to be a rush, rather than purchasing the land, Dorr entered into an agreement that gave him the right of first refusal. A few years later and without notifying Dorr, the owner gave him until noon one day to exercise his option, for a group of townspeople had acquired the funds to purchase the land. Albert Lynam, Dorr's attorney, informed Dorr and with Dorr's approval exercised the option just minutes before noon. In *The Story of Acadia National Park*, Dorr wrote, "The spring was mine, and became, as it proved, one of the foundation stones on which the Park was built." This area Dorr named Sieur de Monts Spring.

Beginning around 1880, village improvement groups in Bar Harbor, Northeast Harbor, and Seal Harbor along with path makers began a series of initiatives to conserve important landmarks in island towns and to take steps to ensure not only adequate water and sewer services but also access to the various summits on Mount Desert Island.

A founding member of the Bar Harbor Village Improvement Association (VIA), Dorr, beginning in the late 1880s, purchased numerous tracts of land around Champlain Mountain and Beaver Dam Pool, along Schooner Head Road, Cromwell Brook, and Great Meadow—all areas near or leading to Sieur de Monts Spring.

Along with Bar Harbor VIA members, Dorr built or oversaw construction of a number of biking and walking paths throughout these lands. The 2006 cultural landscape study *Pathmakers* details not only paths leading from the villages of Bar Harbor, Seal Harbor, and Northeast Harbor but also paths or trails up the island's mountains. In addition to Dorr's purchasing lands, many wealthy summer residents did so as well, and many of these were deeded to HCTPR and then in 1916 and subsequent years to the federal government.

In January 1913, Dorr was at his home in Boston when Lynam called him to tell him that some Bar Harbor residents had introduced a bill in the state legislature to revoke HCTPR's charter. Dorr took the night train to Augusta; once there, he went immediately to the Augusta House, where members gathered. "As it chanced, my friend, the Hon. John A. Peters of Ellsworth, was Speaker of the House that year. . . . I told him what had brought me down and he took the matter up at once with interest, realizing its importance. He made me at home in his rooms at the hotel, where his friends and members of the House came to talk the business of the session over."

Dorr and Peters talked with members who "might have influence in the matter" and talked so convincingly that when the bill came before the House committee, Dorr had the support of members, including the representative from Bar Harbor, who said he did not favor the bill but had introduced it at the request of some constituents.

This incident as well as the earlier incident regarding the purchase of the 10-acre tract at Sieur de Monts made Dorr and others increasingly aware that HCTPR lands needed federal protection. To make the lands appear more attractive to the federal government, Dorr began to build memorial paths at Sieur de Monts Spring. Four of the six paths were funded by women, and two honored women. The Jesup Path, created in honor of Morris K. and Maria DeWitt Jesup, was designed to provide easy access from the village of Bar Harbor to Sieur de Monts.

In the following three years, Dorr drew on his many personal connections. He went to Washington shortly after Woodrow Wilson's inauguration and stayed at the home of Gifford Pinchot, chief of the US Forest Service under Theodore Roosevelt. The Pinchots gave a reception for incoming members of Wilson's cabinet, and Dorr met Wilson "under pleasantest conditions."

In the spring of 1914, Dorr returned to Washington with deeds and maps showing the lands the trustees wanted the government to accept. There was no National Park Service, but there was the

Public Lands Commission. Dorr brought along Edward Howe Forbush, the well-known Massachusetts state ornithologist, to make a case for the importance of these lands for sea and land birds.

The executive secretary of the Public Land Commission was no other than Frank Bond, another well-known ornithologist. Forbush was also an old friend of T.S. Palmer of the Department of Agriculture, a savvy legislative contact who felt it was an inopportune time to ask for park status when Congress was considering bills to establish the National Park Service. Instead, Palmer suggested that Dorr pursue federal recognition under the National Monuments Act—a designation that does not require Congressional approval and only needs the approval of the cabinet member proposing the designation. In this case, it was Secretary of the Interior Franklin Lane, whom Dorr "had met so pleasantly the year before."

Despite Lane's support, it took Dorr two more years and considerable political involvement to have the Sieur de Monts National Monument approved. Yellowstone, which was established in 1872, and other parks and monuments in the West were carved out of federally owned and contiguous lands. Dorr and the trustees of HCTPR were offering the government lands that had been privately purchased and were not contiguous. And there was an additional factor: monuments fell under the jurisdiction of the agency that managed the lands where the monument was located. No federal agency managed the lands on Mount Desert Island, although Secretary Lane supported the designation.

Initially, Dorr was pleased by President Wilson's interest in the monument, but he became concerned when two months had elapsed and the president had taken no action. Dorr began to find out why.

As Ronald Epp points out in his biography of Dorr, "Secretary of Agriculture David F. Houston had sent a memo to Wilson opposing the new monument—ostensibly because of the expense . . . Dorr met with Secretary Houston and assured him that he would manage the proposed national monument at the lowest federal salary—a dollar a month!"

On July 8, 1916, that position became Dorr's when Wilson signed a proclamation designating Sieur de Monts Spring a national monument. The HCTPR trustees turned over more than 6,000 acres to the federal government.

In his quest to augment park lands, Dorr worked closely with John D. Rockefeller Jr., who in 1910 purchased 150 acres on Barr Hill in Seal Harbor; the property included a 99-room cottage, The Eyrie. Rockefeller's father had built carriage roads at his home in Ohio and at Kykuit, an estate in the Hudson Valley. Rockefeller Jr. had learned road construction from his father and wanted to build carriage roads around The Eyrie. Initially, he built roads on land he owned in Seal Harbor—roads around Barr Hill and along the east and west sides of Little Long Pond. The Seal Harbor roads and path committee appreciated not only the carriage roads but also Rockefeller's membership on the committee and his support of a fund for constructing and maintaining paths.

But Rockefeller envisioned a more extensive carriage road system. Dorr and Eliot recognized the value these roads would have. Since some roads would cross land owned by HCTPR, Rockefeller sought and gained the approval of the trustees with a caveat: They would be constructed and maintained at Rockefeller's expense, and he would have no legal rights.

Over 27 years, Rockefeller developed a 57-mile carriage road system—a project that not only provided the public with easier access to interior regions of Acadia but gave testament to Rockefeller's ethic that private money should be used to foster conservation and public enjoyment.

In 1919, Sieur de Monts National Monument became Lafayette National Park, the first national park in the East, and with the new designation its size doubled, for the trustees added an additional 5,000 acres. The name *Lafayette* was chosen in recognition of the alliance and friendship between France and the United States.

Ten years later, Dorr was involved in negotiations to acquire the Schoodic Peninsula. The trustees purchased one-third of the property, while the remaining two-thirds were donated by John Moore's two daughters, Faith and Ruth Moore (Lady Lee) after her marriage to Arthur Lee. Dorr, however, encountered two obstacles: the daughters, who were living in England, objected to the French name, and the original articles of incorporation did not allow the park to acquire land outside of

Mount Desert Island (MDI). When Dorr discussed these obstacles with Louis Cramton (R-MI), chairman of the House Appropriations Committee for the Department of the Interior—who with his wife was Dorr's houseguest in 1928—Cramton said he did not see any obstacles. He instructed Dorr to have his representative introduce legislation allowing the park to acquire land beyond MDI and to change the name to Acadia National Park, the old Native American name for the area.

Until his death in 1944, Dorr labored to improve park lands and to extend Acadia's holdings—efforts that depleted his extensive inheritance. Shortly after Dorr turned 80, he again traveled to Washington. The government had funds to purchase land that had no agricultural value and that people could no longer afford to keep as a result of the Depression. With this funding, Dorr acquired 5,000 acres on the western side of Mount Desert Island. In addition, Dorr secured three Civilian Conservation Corps (CCC) camps, two on MDI and one in Ellsworth—the latter camp worked primarily on Schoodic. Under the supervision of technical staff, in Acadia the CCC built Blackwoods and Seawall Campgrounds, cleared brush and opened vistas, and built gravel truck roads, connector trails, shelters, picnic areas, and trails. These trails included the Ocean Path from Sand Beach to Otter Cliffs—a long scenic trail rebuilt in conjunction with the reconstruction of Ocean Drive.

Most histories of Acadia chronicle the contributions of men in acquiring lands, and while these contributions were critical, women also played a pivotal role. Some funded memorial paths, others facilitated Dorr's acquiring land, and still others donated lands. If people were to enjoy the park and to find respite, infrastructure that provided easy access had to be constructed. And public access was a goal of Dorr, Rockefeller, and National Park Service directors Stephen Mather and Arno Cammerer. This book explores the role of women, the activities that characterize people enjoying the park, and the development of infrastructure, particularly the bridges and motor roads.

One

ACADIA'S BEGINNINGS

George Dorr first visited Bar Harbor in 1866, summering at Old Farm from the 1880s and living there year-round from 1914. Dorr travelled extensively, frequently to Washington, to protect the lands he purchased and those given to the Hancock County Trustees of Public Reservations (HCTPR)— lands that in 1916 became the Sieur de Monts National Monument. Dorr used his substantial inheritance to purchase lands for and to build paths in Acadia. (Courtesy of Acadia National Park.)

President Charles W. Eliot

A longtime Northeast Harbor summer resident and president of Harvard, Charles W. Eliot in 1901 invited a group of island residents to join him in discussing ways to preserve the island's natural beauty and to ensure access for both summer and year-round residents. He proposed developing a land trust similar to one his late son had established in Massachusetts. From this meeting the Hancock County Trustees of Public Reservations was born. (Courtesy of Northeast Harbor Library.)

Without John D. Rockefeller Jr.'s financial backing, attention to detail, and commitment to ensuring that residents and visitors could access various sites in what became Acadia National Park, the park as it is today might not have been created. In addition to developing 57 miles of carriage roads, Rockefeller purchased land for, funded, and oversaw construction of much of the 27-mile Park Loop Road and the Paradise Hill Road. (Courtesy of Library of Congress.)

An original incorporator of the Hancock County Trustees of Public Reservations, its second president, and a Maine Supreme Court chief justice, Luere B. Deasey drafted the language to incorporate HCTPR and to ensure its tax-free status. As a local resident and much-admired public figure, Deasey played a pivotal role in explaining and reconciling the competing concerns of local and summer residents. (Courtesy of Acadia National Park.)

In 1909, when the owner of a significant piece of land decided to sell that land without notifying Dorr, who held an option to buy it, A.H. Lynam, Dorr's attorney, purchased the land and put the title in Dorr's name. Lynam's efforts saved the property from being commercially developed—property later named Sieur de Monts Spring that became the nucleus of the 1916 designated Sieur de Monts National Monument. (Courtesy of Acadia National Park.)

Built in the early 1880s as the Dorr summer home, Old Farm became George Dorr's year-round residence once he sold his Boston home in 1914. Dorr entertained members of Congress and other Washington dignitaries as well as friends and those interested in what became Acadia National Park. (Courtesy of Acadia National Park.)

In May 1908, Bar Harbor summer resident Eliza Homans made the first large donation of land to the Hancock County Trustees of Public Reservations—140 acres that included the Beehive and Bowl. Her gift not only protected land but ensured that her grandchildren would not find "a merry-go-round" built there. She retained the right to use the Beehive Mountain Aqueduct as a public water supply. (Courtesy of Peter Abbot Young.)

The photographer hired by the Satterlee family in 1917 was not the first to capture an image of the Beehive from Sand Beach or Great Head. As art historian Carl Little has noted, the iconic Beehive has inspired numerous artists, including Thomas Cole and Frederick Church—both from the Hudson River School of painters. Carroll Sargent Tyson's 1946 painting also depicts the stream but not the boat in this photograph. (Courtesy of the van Heerden family.)

The Beehive Path, first listed on the 1916 path map, was designed by Rudolph Brunnow, who chaired the Bar Harbor Village Improvement Association (VIA) path committee from 1912 to 1917. This path as well as the Precipice Path, both highly popular, requires hikers to use ladder rungs to ascend cliff faces. (Courtesy of Library of Congress.)

Located just north of the Beehive and at a slightly lower elevation at 419 feet above sea level, the Bowl is a small pond, sometimes called a glacial cirque. First described in 1874, the Bowl Path, which predates the Beehive Path, extends from the Park Loop Road across from Sand Beach to the Bowl. Both those climbing the Beehive or hiking the Bowl trail can enjoy a refreshing swim. (Courtesy of the van Heerden family.)

In addition to donating the Bowl and the Beehive, Eliza Homans also donated the south side of Champlain Mountain, seen here from Otter Creek. Her gift stemmed from her friendship with both Charles Eliot and George Dorr. While she told Eliot he could use her gift as an example, she wished to remain anonymous. (Courtesy of Acadia National Park.)

SCHOODIC PENINSULA - ACADIA NATIONAL PARK

DEDICATED TO THE MEMORY OF

JOHN GODFREY MOORE

1848 ——— 1899

A MAINE MAN WHO LOVED HIS NATIVE STATE, WHEREIN HE
SPENT, WITH HIS FAMILY, SOME OF THE HAPPIEST DAYS OF HIS
LIFE.   HE OWNED SCHOODIC PENINSULA, BUILT THE FIRST
ROAD UPON IT AND OPENED IT TO THE PUBLIC IN THE YEAR
1897

Acquiring land on Schoodic Peninsula began with George Dorr's sitting near Louise Leeds, the widow of John Godfrey Moore, at a dinner. Moore, a native of Steuben, went to New York as a young man to make his fortune. After his death, his widow and two daughters inherited his lands on Schoodic Peninsula. Mrs. Leeds offered Dorr her share and recommended the daughters donate theirs, although expanding Acadia to the mainland required Congressional approval since the legislation establishing Acadia specified the government could accept lands only on Mount Desert Island. When Dorr discovered Representative Cramton, chairman of the House Appropriations Committee, and his wife might visit the park, he invited them to stay at Old Farm. Cramton suggested modifying the original legislation to include lands on the mainland—a modification he agreed to promote. (Above, courtesy of Thomas Gonye; left, courtesy of Acadia National Park.)

In 1900, J. Pierpont Morgan gave his daughter Louisa a wedding present—over 100 acres of land that included Great Head and Sand Beach. This 1917 photograph not only shows the expanse of land with the inlet behind Sand Beach but parts of Louisa and Herbert Satterlee's home, built in 1911 and called Satterlee Field. On the top left, the Tea House, pictured on pages 20-21, is barely visible. (Courtesy of the van Heerden family.)

On the highest point of Great Head, the Satterlees built this 15-foot-tall teahouse. Herbert Satterlee stands in the doorway waiting to greet guests. Inside was a fireplace as well as a rustic table, chairs, and a ladder that led to the observation deck. The Tea House was damaged in the October 1947 wildfire that swept across 1,788 acres on the east side of Mount Desert Island. (Courtesy of the van Heerden family.)

Taken from one of the windows of the Tea House, this photograph shows the view looking east toward Oak Hill Cliff and Schooner Head. (Courtesy of the van Heerden family.)

From their lawn, the Satterlees viewed Gorham Mountain on the right and Otter Cliffs in the distance. Louisa Satterlee died in 1946 and Herbert Satterlee in 1947. In 1948, their daughters, Eleanor and Mabel, deeded the property to the park in memory of their mother and stipulated a plaque be placed at the entrance to Sand Beach—a beach where the family for many years had welcomed park visitors. (Courtesy of the van Heerden family.)

Two

MEMORIAL PATHS AND SIEUR DE MONTS SPRING

After the 1913 Maine Legislature attempted to revoke the tax-exempt status of the Hancock County Trustees of Public Reservations, George Dorr realized the lands needed federal protection. To enhance their attractiveness to the government, Dorr began developing Sieur de Monts Spring with memorial paths connecting the area with the town and surrounding mountains—four memorial paths were funded by women and two honored women. The Kane Path, constructed in 1915, is graced by an engraved boulder and bronze plaque: "In memory of John Innes Kane, a man of kindness who found his happiness in giving others pleasure. 1913." (Courtesy of Malek Hinnawi.)

Constructed of large flat stones, the Kane Path, which George Dorr began in 1913, runs along the west side of the Tarn. Annie Schermerhorn Kane gave funds to construct the path in memory of her late husband, John Innes Kane, who had been a member of the path committee of the Bar Harbor VIA. (Courtesy of Acadia National Park.)

In this photograph taken around 1916, Annie Schermerhorn Kane walks along the Kane Path with George Dorr, who designed the path that connects two Dorr Mountain paths—the Ladder Path and the Canon Brook Path—with the Tarn and Sieur de Monts Spring. (Courtesy of Acadia National Park.)

Annie Schermerhorn Kane and her sister Fannie Schermerhorn Bridgham, along with their husbands, contributed funds to purchase land on Dorr Mountain. The two sisters also donated the lake and surrounding land at Lakewood. Landscape gardener Beatrix Farrand designed a memorial bridge at Lakewood honoring them. Today, only remnants of the bridge remain. Beaver dams caused water levels to rise in nearby ponds and streams, and the rising water levels damaged the bridge. (Courtesy of Bar Harbor Historical Society collection.)

In 1913, George Dorr began another memorial path, the Kurt Diederich Climb—a steep .4-mile path that was funded by Diederich's aunt, Enid Hunt Slater. Diederich died from anesthesia in 1913. The name of the path is engraved on the sixth step. In the Acadia National Park archives is a bronze plaque: "In memory of Kurt Diederich, Who loved these mountains, 1913." (Courtesy of Malek Hinnawi.)

After her mother died in 1911, Elsa Diederich and her father, Kurt, moved from London to Washington, DC, where they lived with his aunt, Enid Hunt Slater. They summered in Bar Harbor at her Bowling Green cottage. Park records indicate this photograph was most likely taken around 1916. (Courtesy of Acadia National Park.)

One of the early memorial paths, the Homans Path, developed by George Dorr in 1915, honors Eliza Lothrop Homans, who, in 1908, made the first substantial gift of land to the Hancock County Trustees of Public Reservations—141 acres. As this photograph shows, the path is characterized by its large stone steps and lintels—stones that are placed across a path to form an arch or bridge. (Courtesy of Sheridan Steele.)

Completed in 1915, the Beachcroft Path honors C. Morton Smith, a Philadelphia industrialist and a summer resident of Bar Harbor. His widow, Anna Warren Ingersoll Smith, not only funded construction of the path but in the 1920s established an endowment for its maintenance since she felt the park was not properly caring for it. A stone marks the beginning of the path across from the Tarn on Route 3. (Courtesy of Sam Putnam.)

Like the Kane Path, the Beachcroft Path uses uniquely long sections of flat stones that aid footing while climbing up a mountain. George Dorr credits Andrew Liscomb, superintendent of paths for the Bar Harbor VIA, with designing the layout of many of the surrounding memorial paths and supervising a construction crew of trail builders and masons. Dorr and Liscomb chose narrow, winding routes with boulders and open ledges. (Courtesy of Northeast Harbor Library.)

One of George Dorr's favorite paths, the Emery Path, built in 1916, was funded by Lela Anson in memory of her first husband, John Emery, a member of the Bar Harbor VIA path committee and a successful real estate developer in Cincinnati. In 1934, the Civilian Conservation Corps (CCC) made improvements to the path. (Courtesy of Bar Harbor Historical Society collection.)

Hiking the Emery Path opens up stunning views of the ocean and the Great Meadow. By mid-May, the meadow is ablaze with purple rhodora (*Rhododendron canadense*), a native plant of Acadia. By mid-September, the bright red leaves of the swamp maple (*Acer rubrum*) at the south end of the meadow, near the Hemlock Road, usher in autumn on Mount Desert Island. (Courtesy of Bar Harbor Historical Society collection.)

Once autumn transitions to late autumn and early winter, the Great Meadow takes on various hues. Without sunlight on the mountains surrounding the meadow, the mountains become dark while the meadow has golden tones. Even the waters of Cromwell Brook as it meanders through the meadow look cold but are not yet iced over. (Courtesy of Ashleigh Conti/Friends of Acadia.)

Moving into the Turrets, a massive three-story granite structure designed by Bruce Price, signified the Emerys' arrival as important members of the Bar Harbor summer community. The building, which took 100 workers two years to construct and cost $100,000, was a wedding present from John Emery to his 18-year-old bride, Lela Alexander. From 1895 until his death in 1908, Emery summered there with his wife and five children. (Courtesy of College of the Atlantic.)

This 1904 photograph of the Turrets depicts the finished building. The granite for this building was quarried near Eagle Lake. Although Bruce Price, the architect of the Chateau Frontenac, designed other buildings in Bar Harbor, the Turrets is the only extant example of his work. Today, the Turrets is an administrative and classroom building of College of the Atlantic. (Courtesy of College of the Atlantic.)

This memorial path, one Dorr constructed, honors Jacob Henry Schiff (pictured at left), an international banker and philanthropist who funded a number of trails in Acadia. According to *Pathmakers*, there is no known plaque or engraved stone. A heavily used trail, the Schiff Path connects four lower trails on Dorr Mountain. (Above, courtesy of Acadia National Park; left, courtesy of *The World's Work*, Internet Archive.)

Beginning in the 1890s, George Dorr purchased lands around Schooner Head, Cromwell Harbor, the Great Meadow, and Sieur de Monts Spring to develop bike and walking paths so residents and visitors could easily access trails and points of interest in the park. The Jesup Path, built by Dorr and the Bar Harbor VIA, led from Bar Harbor to Sieur de Monts Spring and then to the Tarn. The path honors Morris K. Jesup and Maria DeWitt Jesup, two longtime summer residents. In addition to contributing to Robert Perry's Arctic expedition, Morris founded the VIA. Maria built Bar Harbor's Jesup Memorial Library in memory of her husband and in 1918 gave $50,000 to endow the library. The plaque reads: "In memory of Morris K. and Maria DeWitt Jesup, Lovers of this island." (Right, courtesy of Ashley Conti/Friends of Acadia; below, courtesy of Malek Hinnawi.)

The Jesup Path ends at the Tarn. This view is looking south with the stepping stones Dorr built visible at the edge of the Tarn. (Courtesy of Acadia National Park.)

These stones that George Dorr built across the north end of the Tarn allow walkers or hikers coming from the Tarn parking area, the Wild Gardens Path, or the Beachcroft Path to cross over to the Jesup and Kane Paths on the west side of the Tarn. (Courtesy of Earl Brechlin.)

After acquiring the land between the Great Meadow and the Tarn—land that included a natural spring—Dorr built an octagonal structure with a tile roof over the spring. On a nearby rock, he carved "Sweet Waters of Acadia." Water from the spring flowed into a nearby pool and reflects Dorr's original design. (Courtesy of Acadia National Park.)

Katherine Pulitzer and her son visit the pool at Sieur de Monts Spring. The stepping stones behind them lead to the memorial paths. While at times there were large gatherings at Sieur de Monts, there were also times then—and now—for individuals to come to the area and enjoy both the natural and built features. (Courtesy of Acadia National Park.)

In addition to developing the seven memorial paths—all of which were in proximity to Sieur de Monts Spring—George Dorr emphasized the area as a gathering place, the nucleus of the newly established Sieur de Monts Spring National Monument. Regularly people gathered there for lectures, celebrations, and school outings such as the one enjoyed by children from St. Joseph's School in Bar Harbor. (Courtesy of Acadia National Park.)

Three

CONSTRUCTING CADILLAC MOUNTAIN ROAD

Long before anyone thought of constructing a motor road up Cadillac Mountain, the Brewer family, who owned much of the mountain, including the summit, built and rebuilt a buckboard road that was popular with pedestrians or, as in this 1888 photograph, for pulling a sled-like wagon. The road also provided access for those staying at the Summit Tavern and for staff at the US Coastal Survey's Triangulation Station, a station that takes readings for making accurate maps. (Courtesy of Southwest Harbor Public Library.)

Automobiles were not allowed on the island until 1915, and by 1919, many were discussing building a motor road up the highest peak on the Eastern Seaboard. John D. Rockefeller Jr. acquired considerable land and began constructing a road. After grading about 500 feet, Rockefeller deeded the land to the park. The National Park Service (NPS) announced the project in 1922, but work was delayed when some influential people believed that building a motor road would detract from the wilderness experience and their enjoyment of nature. Citing local support, NPS director Stephen Mather in 1928 authorized the project. Since relatively little grading had been completed by 1928, Mather asked the Bureau of Public Roads (BPR) to take over. BPR engineers not only surveyed possible routes but also made "diagrammatic views" by mapping possible routes on photographs of Cadillac as shown here. (Both, courtesy of Acadia National Park/Leo Grossman Papers, 1927–1944.)

After conducting yet another survey, BPR assigned senior engineer W.J. Anderson and junior engineer Leo Grossman to the project. The engineers retained as much as possible of the existing road from the entrance off the Mountain Road to White Cap, a northwestern spur on Cadillac, approximately one mile from the entrance. The project consisted of two parts: grading, or constructing, and surfacing. (Courtesy of Acadia National Park/Leo Grossman Papers, 1927-1944.)

The low bidder on this first portion of the grading project was Joseph P. McCabe Inc. of Boston with a bid of $146,323.60. According to the final construction report (1930), on August 12, 1929, McCabe moved in a steam shovel, a gas shovel, five trucks, a Caterpillar tractor, five compressors, nine jackhammers, a drill sharpener, and two forges. The report also notes that McCabe barely broke even on this phase. (Courtesy of Acadia National Park/Leo Grossman Papers, 1927-1944.)

Approximately 90 percent of the Cadillac Mountain Road was blasted, and the blasted material was used as fill and to build shoulders. Prior to the blasting, Acadia National Park crew had cleared the land, but the contractor pulled out stumps with power shovels. (Courtesy of Acadia National Park/Leo Grossman Papers, 1927–1944.)

Before rock could be blasted, the construction crew drilled into the rock—an extremely costly and difficult process. McCabe hired blacksmiths to maintain the drills and brought in explosive consultants while BPR sent engineers to assess the project. While the men here with Frank McCabe (center), project superintendent, were not identified by name, the man on the far right may be Dennis Doonan, the dynamite man. (Courtesy of Acadia National Park/Leo Grossman Papers, 1927–1944.)

Working overtime with two other crew members, dynamite man Dennis Doonan, with over 30 years of experience, was fatally injured when a third stick of dynamite was added to the drill hole while they were blasting a ledge near the lower end of the road. Doonan died in the hospital the following day. (Courtesy of Acadia National Park/Leo Grossman Papers, 1927–1944.)

Using a Lorain 75, a gas-powered steam shovel, McCabe's operator is loading large boulders into one of the five dump trucks he initially brought in to use in constructing the Cadillac Mountain Road. (Courtesy of Acadia National Park/Leo Grossman Papers, 1927–1944.)

Once a section was blasted, an engineer walked the area to make recommendations for dispersing rock. (Courtesy of Acadia National Park/Leo Grossman Papers, 1927–1944.)

According to Paul MacQuinn, president of Harold MacQuinn Inc.—a company that worked extensively on Acadia's bridges, carriage roads, and sections of the Loop Road—the vehicle in this photograph appears to have been built specifically for this project in order to move these heavy rocks. His reasoning lies in his never having previously seen a similar vehicle, the use of wagon wheels, and the high placement of the idler gear. While moving blasted rock was generally easy work, one embankment was so steep that the crew used a derrick to construct a 10- to 30-foot-high embankment. (Courtesy of Acadia National Park/Leo Grossman Papers, 1927–1944.)

Crew moved rocks and leveled the blasted area that would become the road itself. The larger boulders were used for guardrails. *The Cultural Landscape Report for the Historic Motor Road System* quotes Grossman: "As wooden or steel cable guide rail did not seem appropriate for this type of road, it was specified that selected boulders should be taken from the excavation." (Courtesy of Acadia National Park/Leo Grossman Papers, 1927–1944.)

These boulders were similar to those lining the motor road from Eagle Lake to Jordan Pond and those lining the extensive carriage road system John D. Rockefeller Jr. built on his private land and parklands. (Courtesy of Acadia National Park/Leo Grossman Papers, 1927–1944.)

On October 13, J.P. McCabe (right) and a friend, Mr. Childs (center), visited the site and met with superintendent Frank McCabe. In the photograph below, an unidentified man but possibly J.P. McCabe views the construction project from one of the coping stones. In the background are some of the offshore islands visible from sections of the motor road and the summit. (Both, courtesy of Acadia National Park/Leo Grossman Papers, 1927-1944.)

On June 17, 1930, BPR engineer Guy Miller authorized extending the mountain road to the summit of Cadillac. (Courtesy of Acadia National Park/Leo Grossman Papers, 1927–1944.)

In December 1930, Charles Peterson, an assistant landscape architect with the National Park Service, came to Acadia to inspect the project. He expressed concern that along portions of the road, the contractor had not cleaned up excess rock—rock that is evident on the left side of this photograph. By the time the road was dedicated in 1932, park crews had removed the excess rock. (Courtesy of Acadia National Park/Leo Grossman Papers, 1927–1944.)

Both of these photographs show how the construction crew marked out the shoulders and the placement of coping stones as guardrails. The coping stones were approximately four feet apart. As the photograph below indicates, the road was passable even before final paving. (Both, courtesy of Acadia National Park/Leo Grossman Papers, 1927–1944.)

By November 1930, the grading portion of the Cadillac Mountain Road was complete. BPR then developed specifications for paving or surfacing the road. Green and Wilson of Waterville, Maine, submitted the low bid of $60,760.62. Initially, Green and Wilson lengthened culverts and improved visibility in some areas along the Cadillac Mountain Road. (Courtesy of Acadia National Park/ Leo Grossman Papers, 1927–1944.)

This crushing and screening plant allowed surfacing crews to crush blasted granite to form paving aggregate for the historic road system. Because granite throughout the park varies considerably in color, paving along sections of the historic park roads also varied—variation that allowed blending with the landscape. On the Cadillac Mountain Road, the aggregate came from a blasted section of pink granite about two-thirds of the way up the road. (Courtesy of Acadia National Park/ Leo Grossman Papers, 1927–1944.)

The above photograph shows the various layers involved in paving the Cadillac Mountain Road, while the image below shows the finished road before paving. Once paving was completed in October 1931, cars were allowed to go up the mountain during daylight hours. Park records indicate that on opening day in October 1931, a total of 3,000 people in 800 cars made the trip up the mountain. The official dedication of the $350,000 road occurred on July 23, 1932. (Both, courtesy of Acadia National Park/Leo Grossman Papers, 1927–1944.)

901K-14)(7-27-35-2:40P)(12-2000) MT. CADALLIC, ME.

This aerial photograph aptly depicts the circuitous route and the gradual grades that characterize the Cadillac Mountain Road from its beginning just off the Eagle Lake to Jordan Pond Road (often called the Lower Mountain Road) to the summit of Cadillac at an elevation of 1,530 feet. Following his June 1922 inspection trip, assistant NPS director Arno Cammerer urged NPS director Stephen Mather to authorize construction of a road. "In my opinion," wrote Cammerer, "a road up Cadillac Mountain will not be equaled anywhere in the United States for its combination of mountain massing, valley, inland lakes, and ocean and should be given when built a distinctive name that will identify it as a national scenic road and give it individuality throughout the world." (Courtesy of Maine Historic Preservation Commission.)

George Dorr, Charles Eliot, and John D. Rockefeller Jr. advocated building carriage and motor roads as a way of opening the park and its many vistas to everyone. Similarly, one of the objectives in building the Cadillac Mountain Road—an objective supported by NPS director Stephen Mather and assistant director Arno Cammerer—was to give all, but particularly those who physically could not climb Cadillac, an opportunity to see the panoramic views from the summit as well as vistas along the road—vistas such as this one of Bar Harbor and the offshore islands (above) and an elevated view facing north (below). (Above, courtesy of Acadia National Park; below, courtesy of Library of Congress.)

Building this road required extensive blasting, as shown in this photograph aptly named "Major Road Cut." Bureau of Public Road engineers had to ensure that the road rose gradually so that the grade or incline did not exceed seven percent. (Courtesy of Library of Congress.)

Not all views from the Cadillac Mountain Road are of offshore islands, Eagle Lake, Baker Island, Bar Harbor, or of mountains and ocean. Sometimes when driving up the road on foggy days, visitors get above the fog bank. The summit and upper reaches of the road are bathed in sunlight, and one looks out on what appears to be a sea of fog—a truly magical experience. (Courtesy of Acadia National Park.)

In the mid-1930s, the park ranger-naturalist wrote a guide, "Are You Driving Down Cadillac Mt?" At 1.1 miles from the end of the loop on Cadillac's summit, notes the guide, is a view of Eagle Lake and beyond it Aunt Betty's Pond. "Both the basins containing these bodies of water were scoured out by the glacier many thousands of years ago when all the surrounding country was overridden by a great ice sheet from the north," stated the guide. (Courtesy of Acadia National Park.)

One of the immediate concerns after the road opened was inadequate parking at the summit. In August 1932, the McCabe construction company received a $13,000 contract to increase the number of parking spaces, and this 1932 photograph shows the enlarged parking area. While some additional parking has been added over the years, the core area looks essentially the same as this view. (Courtesy of Acadia National Park.)

From the parking area at Cadillac's summit, there are trails circling the summit and various places to just sit on the rocks and look out over the ocean and offshore islands. (Courtesy of Acadia National Park.)

Ascending Cadillac for ranger-naturalist Maurice Sullivan meant putting chains on his tires. In a 1991 interview with the *Bar Harbor Times*, Sullivan, who began working in Acadia in 1936 as part of the CCC program, recalled overnight trips up Cadillac with visitors—"building campfires, singing songs, sleeping under the stars, and being the first people in the country to see the sun rise." (Courtesy of Acadia National Park.)

Today, ascending the Cadillac Mountain Road in winter requires hiking up the road. While throughout the 1930s the road was regularly plowed, packed snow and ice did not deter some intrepid drivers. (Courtesy of Southwest Harbor Public Library.)

Although snow and ice can make driving up Cadillac in winter difficult, those reaching the summit were well rewarded with a view of snow-covered conifers, the Porcupine Islands, and Bar Harbor. (Courtesy of Southwest Harbor Public Library.)

A July 1933 ranger program encourages visitors "to see the sun rise from the highest point above the north Atlantic coast. Bring and cook breakfast if desired—fireplaces and wood available for that purpose. [Take a] short Naturalist-guided walk over the new summit trail after sunrise. Mountain Road open at 3:30 for this occasion," wrote ranger-naturalist Arthur Stupa. (Courtesy of Acadia National Park.)

While the same program guide lists evening campfire programs at the new campground amphitheater at Blackwoods, by 1939 when this photograph was taken, there were regular evening campfire programs on Cadillac. (Courtesy of Acadia National Park.)

Four

HISTORIC ROADS
AND BRIDGES

With the development of towns on Mount Desert Island in the 18th century, the settlers used old footpaths to link villages. The *Cultural Landscape Report for the Historic Road System* notes footpaths were widened to accommodate wagons and logging carriages. By 1777, Schooner Head Road extended from Cromwell Cove in Bar Harbor to Sand Beach. By the 1880s, a number of summer "cottages" dotted Schooner Head Road; year-round and summer residents took carriage rides to enjoy scenic Ocean Drive. (Courtesy of Southwest Harbor Public Library.)

The Schooner Head Path, a village connector path constructed by the Bar Harbor VIA, is depicted on the 1901 path map. The 3.5-mile path may have been improved by the Civilian Conservation Corps in the 1930s. Although sections of the path were abandoned, this path has been rebuilt with new trail signs and extends from Compass Harbor to Schooner Head. (Courtesy of Acadia National Park.)

In the 1890s, the town of Bar Harbor constructed an unpaved scenic road, Ocean Drive, paralleling the eastern shoreline. An 1896 map shows the road extending from the end of Schooner Head Road at Sand Beach to Otter Cliff Road. The Beehive is in the background. (Courtesy of Bar Harbor Historical Society collection.)

ROAD NEAR SAND BEACH—BEEHIVE MOUNTAIN IN BACKGROUND

While this photograph is undated, Ocean Drive has acquired guardrails. Otter Cliffs is toward the top right. In 1929, John D. Rockefeller Jr. funded a 500-foot demonstration project near Thunder Hole to show how all of Ocean Drive could be reconstructed. Between 1933 and 1934, Rockefeller funded reconstruction of Ocean Drive from Sand Beach to Otter Cliffs. (Courtesy of Maine Historic Preservation Commission.)

The note on the back of this photograph indicates it was taken by Pulpit Rock, which is just north of Thunder Hole on Ocean Drive. (Courtesy of Bar Harbor Historical Society collection.)

In this 1908 photograph, telephone poles and lines have been added to Ocean Drive as it nears the junction of Otter Cliffs and Otter Cliff Road. The tall structure in the top right is the tower for the Navy's radio station that is on the other side of the peninsula comprising Otter Point. (Courtesy of Bar Harbor Historical Society collection.)

This picture shows an early version of the Ocean Path, a coastal trail in Bar Harbor's VIA district. First described by Clara Martin in her 1874 guidebook *Mount Desert on the Coast of Maine*, the path is not apparent in the earlier photographs of Ocean Drive. The date of this photograph is unknown, but it clearly shows a more developed road than in previous images. (Courtesy of Southwest Harbor Public Library.)

The Mountain Road, Acadia National Park   Mt. Desert Island, Me.

The 18.5-mile Park Loop Road was constructed in noncontiguous sections between 1922 and 1958 with the Paradise Hill section not connected until 1953. The first section, the Mountain Road built between 1922 and 1927, ran from Eagle Lake Road to Jordan Pond House and was constructed in two phases. The first extended from Eagle Lake Road to what is now the intersection with Cadillac Mountain Road offering views of Eagle Lake. (Courtesy of Earl Brechlin.)

SCENE ON CADILLAC MOUNTAIN ROAD, ACADIA NATIONAL PARK,
MT. DESERT ISLAND, MAINE

Driving north from the Jordan Pond House to Bubble Pond, one views Jordan Pond on the left and the South Bubble in the distance. George Dorr advocated building the Mountain Road not only to provide shorter access to the Jordan Pond House but also to "enable our rangers to pass readily between the northern and southern side of our mountain range, for wildlife and woods protection." (Courtesy of MDI Historical Society collections.)

This 1926 photograph shows one of the crews who built the road from Eagle Lake Road to Bubble Pond. The photograph was taken about .25 miles north of Bubble Pond. (Courtesy of Bar Harbor Historical Society collection.)

Designed by Charles Stoughton and built between 1934 and 1936, this triple-arch bridge spans the Seaside Path, the Stanley Brook Road, and Stanley Brook. Frederick Law Olmsted Jr. consulted with John D. Rockefeller Jr. to ensure that the scale of the Stanley Brook Road was appropriate for this narrow valley. Olmsted also designed the Seal Harbor end of the road to showcase the dramatic views of the harbor. (Courtesy of Library of Congress.)

The central arch stands 23.5 feet above the road while the arch over the trail is almost 10 feet tall and the arch over the stream is 14.6 feet. In a letter to Olmsted, Rockefeller noted that since he owned the land on both sides of the road, he would not need anyone's consent to build this road and bridge—both of which he deeded to the park. (Courtesy of Library of Congress.)

Unlike most of the carriage road bridges, the stone parapet on the Stanley Brook Bridge is pointed. Completed in 1936, this bridge carries the Barr Hill–Day Mountain carriage road over the Stanley Brook Road, Seaside Path, and Stanley Brook. In the upper left is the traditional carriage road sign listing various options from that point and the distance of each. (Courtesy of Library of Congress.)

First shown on a 1903 path map, the Seaside Path, constructed by the Seal Harbor Village Improvement Society, extended from the Jordan Pond House to the Seaside Inn in Seal Harbor just across from the beach. Originally a boardinghouse in the 1870s, the inn expanded in the 1890s. This path provided easy access for guests not only to the Jordan Pond House but also to several trails. (Courtesy of Maine Historic Preservation Commission.)

This caravan is approaching Otter Cliffs. In 1936, Frederick Law Olmsted Jr. designed this grade separation to ensure that drivers in either direction would have unobstructed ocean views. Viewed from the water, the structure looks as if it is part of the cliff. In the 1980s, the Loop Road from Kebo Mountain Road to Day Mountain Road, including Otter Cliff Road, was changed to one way. (Courtesy of Acadia National Park.)

This two-tiered structure was built over the former naval radio station that in 1935 moved to the Schoodic Peninsula. At both Otter Point and Schoodic, there was a clear transatlantic radio signal. The Navy stipulated that it would not move unless the new site provided such a signal, and John D. Rockefeller Jr. had said he would not continue the road around Otter Point unless the station was relocated. (Courtesy of Library of Congress.)

The grade separation at Otter Cliffs includes the two-tiered separation for the road and a third separation for those walking along the Ocean Path—a path that begins by Sand Beach, passes Thunder Hole, and extends around all of Otter Point. Along this path is a memorial marker commemorating John D. Rockefeller Jr. for his many contributions to Acadia. (Courtesy of Library of Congress.)

Constructing a motor road across Otter Cove was challenging, for engineers had to consider high seas and tidal flow. Several engineers studied the feasibility of different designs, but all failed. In the late 1920s, John D. Rockefeller Jr. hired Frederick Law Olmsted's firm. Once the $500,000 funding was secured, Rockefeller deeded the land for the road to the government. Constructed entirely of masonry, the causeway had three bays so that water could freely flow in and out of Otter Cove at low and high tides. When completed in 1939, Rockefeller wrote Olmsted commending him on the project: "The causeway looks as if it had always been there, so naturally is it related to the surrounding country, while the curve only adds to its beauty." (Courtesy of Library of Congress.)

In the late 1930s, the park constructed the Kebo Mountain Road, connecting the Jordan Pond/Eagle Lake Road with the Harden Farm Road near the Kebo Valley Golf Club. The road was subsequently extended past the Great Meadow (the view shown here), the Sieur de Monts area, and Bear Brook Campground to Beaver Dam Pond. But the final segment was not constructed until the mid-1950s when Pauline Palmer donated her property on the west side of Schooner Head Road. This gift allowed the park to construct not only the final segment of the Loop Road but also the Champlain overlook and the Precipice parking lot. (Courtesy of Library of Congress.)

PARADISE HILL ROAD — BAR HARBOR, MAINE

Although surveyed in the mid-1930s, construction on the 3.5-mile Paradise Hill Road did not begin until December 1940. It was completed by October 1941. The road, which extended from Hulls Cove to the intersection with the Jordan Pond/Eagle Lake Road, was not usable. Because of World War II, funds for constructing three bridges—spanning Duck Brook, New Eagle Lake Road, and Eagle Lake Road (Route 233)—were not allocated. (Courtesy of Bar Harbor Historical Society collection.)

Constructed between 1951 and 1953 at a cost of $366,000, this 402-foot-long triple-arch bridge spanning Duck Brook is the longest bridge in Acadia National Park and, at the time of construction, was the longest one in the eastern United States. (Courtesy of Bar Harbor Historical Society collection.)

Three semielliptical arches support the bridge. Although not readily perceptible in this photograph, the center arch, with a span of 95 feet, is six feet higher than the side arches. Constructing this bridge required 4,000 pounds of concrete, 2,000 tons of reinforced steel, and 1,100 cubic yards of stone. The granite for the bridge came from Hall Quarry on the west side of the island. (Courtesy of Library of Congress.)

These columns or barrels, visible on the right side of this photograph, provide critical support for the bridge. Construction workers used ladders, which were left inside the bridge, to do necessary work. Since these had rotted, a construction crew spent most of the summer in 2022 building a catwalk around the upper part of the interior in order to check the status of the bridge and make any necessary repairs. (Courtesy of Library of Congress.)

John D. Rockefeller Jr. played a critical role in the construction of two bridges over Duck Brook. He constructed the carriage road bridge on land he owned. Like the bridge on the Paradise Hill Road, this carriage road bridge, connecting the Witch Hole and Paradise Hill loops with an access road from Bar Harbor, is tripled arched. Considered to be the most sophisticated of the 16 carriage road bridges, the deck provides views toward Frenchman Bay and the Duck Brook ravine. A stairway, not shown in this photograph, allows visitors to access the brook and view the bridge from below. (Courtesy of Library of Congress.)

John D. Rockefeller Jr. purchased the land for the Paradise Hill Road and the bridge. Aware that the impending war in Europe would require funding to shift toward the war effort, Rockefeller advocated for contracts to be advertised and awarded before the United States became an active participant. But actual construction was delayed until 1950. The two bridges show Duck Brook as it flows from Eagle Lake, the source of Bar Harbor's water supply, and empties into Frenchman Bay. (Courtesy of Library of Congress.)

At Bar Harbor's March 1940 town meeting, voters agreed to allow bridges to be constructed over the New Eagle Lake Road and Eagle Lake Road (Route 233). Town officials also agreed to relocate Eagle Lake Road and to transfer ownership of New Eagle Lake Road to the federal government. Today, New Eagle Lake Road is called Duck Brook Road, a portion of which is open only to walkers and bikers. (Courtesy of Library of Congress.)

This bridge just .1 mile north of the Cadillac Mountain entrance to Acadia on Route 233 provides access to the Paradise Hill Road and the Park Loop Road. Like the New Eagle Lake Road Bridge, construction of this bridge required approval from the Town of Bar Harbor. Although that approval was granted in 1940, World War II and a subsequent lack of funds delayed construction until 1951. (Courtesy of Bar Harbor Historical Society collection.)

The contract for this bridge as well as the two other bridges on the Paradise Hill Road was awarded to Harold MacQuinn Inc. of Hulls Cove. MacQuinn employed over 50 men for this project, which cost $152,000. George O'Neil of Bar Harbor was the resident engineer for the Bureau of Public Roads. Because of cold weather, work on both bridges was suspended during the winter months. When completed, this large stone-faced, reinforced concrete bridge was 99 feet long with a span of 42 feet, 9 inches. The stone used in the facing and for the arch is native pink granite. (Both, courtesy of Bar Harbor Historical Society collection.)

Constructed in 1928 at a cost of $70,627—more than $22,000 over estimate—a Gothic-style bridge separated Route 233 from the carriage roads connecting the Eagle Lake loop to the Witch Hole Pond loop. Anticipating increased traffic, town officials asked John D. Rockefeller Jr. to widen the bridge from 21 to 27 feet—a move that would have increased the price by $4,000. Rockefeller refused. (Courtesy of Harold MacQuinn Inc.)

As traffic on Route 233 increased and trucks became larger, the bridge proved to be too narrow. In the 1970s, the National Park Service and Maine Department of Transportation recognized the bridge was both a historical structure and a safety concern. In August 1974, the contract to widen the bridge was awarded to Harold MacQuinn Inc. The original plan was to take down the bridge stone by stone and then reconstruct it. But when they began stripping the barrel or core, MacQuinn came up with the idea of separating the arches from the barrel by first lifting and then moving the north arch. Before actually doing this, he tested the idea to be sure it would work. At MacQuinn's Hulls Cove yard, workers inserted ball bearings—the small balls seen here on the inside of the right track—into steel channels or tracks. (Both, courtesy of Harold MacQuinn Inc.)

In the above photograph, the engineer instructs crew as they loaded pieces of granite onto the steel channels. The crew added granite blocks weighing approximately 20 tons to determine how many steel channels they would need to move a 700-ton arch, for the channels bear the weight of the arch. This mock test showed that using channels and ball bearings would allow the crew to separate the bridge's arch from the barrel and move it 13 feet horizontally. (Both, courtesy of Harold MacQuinn Inc.)

Near the top of this photograph on the left is a wedge that adds pressure to aid the workers who are using a vibrating hammer and drill to separate the arch from the barrel or core of the bridge. (Courtesy of Harold MacQuinn Inc.)

To aid in separating the north arch from the bridge's barrel, one of the crew burned through the granite so that the steel channels with the ball bearings could be inserted. This step aided the crew in gaining access to the inside of the wall. (Courtesy of Harold MacQuinn Inc.)

The crew constructed a form for the steel channels and ball bearings. Once these were in place and the bridge jacked up, crews then added a concrete form that not only covered the channels but also indicated where the bottom of the bridge would rest. Paul MacQuinn, president of Harold MacQuinn Inc., called this an important step since it determined the grade and indicated the placement for each steel rail. (Both, courtesy of Harold MacQuinn Inc.)

Once the arch was separated from the barrel, it was ready to be moved. Near the top left of this photograph, one can see the scored concrete—markings that resulted from drilling. Moving the arch 13 feet to the north required patience and precision. Men were positioned on each side of the steel channels. When the foreman blew a whistle, they moved three steps to the north and stopped. They repeated this process until the north arch was in its new position—a process that took three days. (Courtesy of Harold MacQuinn Inc.)

When the arch was safely moved, the MacQuinn crew then expanded the core structure or barrel with granite from Hall Quarry on the west side of Mount Desert Island. They so closely matched the original granite that the slight difference in color is only apparent if one looks closely. Once this was completed, the deck of the bridge was repaved. (Courtesy of Harold MacQuinn Inc.)

One goal of Harold MacQuinn and his son Ronnie, who oversaw this project, was to keep one lane of traffic open throughout the process, for this east-west road is the major connection between Bar Harbor and the west side of Mount Desert Island. (Courtesy of Harold MacQuinn Inc.)

Federal Highway Administration

The Highway And Its Environment Tenth Annual Awards 1977

Outstanding Sympathetic Treatment of Historic, Cultural, or Natural Environment

Eagle Lake Bridge in Acadia National Park

First Place

Harold MacQuinn, Inc.
Bar Harbor, Maine

_____
Administrator

_____
Secretary of Transportation

When the park and the Maine Department of Transportation recognized that the Route 233 bridge over the Eagle Lake carriage road had to be widened, one of their main concerns was preserving the historical integrity of the bridge. In 1977, the Federal Highway Administration presented Harold MacQuinn Inc. with a first place award for the company's "outstanding sympathetic treatment of historic, cultural, or natural environment." Harold MacQuinn (right) went to Washington to accept the award. (Both, courtesy of Harold MacQuinn Inc.)

Harold MacQuinn Inc. received an additional national award—the Associated General Contractors of America Build America Award. This award was accepted by Ronald MacQuinn at the annual Associated General Contractors convention in Washington. After Harold retired, Ron became president. At his death in 2009, his son Paul became president. "Visitors for multiple generations have benefitted immensely from the long-term preservation experience of the MacQuinn family on the historic resources of Acadia," said Keith Johnston, chief of facility management at Acadia. Three generations of MacQuinns have worked on Acadia's carriage roads, bridges, and sections of the Loop Road. (Courtesy of the MacQuinn family.)

Five

RANGERS, NATURALISTS, AND STAFF

In 1937, these four rangers-naturalists, from left to right, John Pierce, Paul Favour, Richard Manville, and Maurice Sullivan, stand under the trees near park headquarters across from the athletic field in Bar Harbor. Their names were written in pencil in the lower left corner. Their uniforms look much heavier than those worn by rangers today. While the hats remain the same, rangers today wear hiking boots, not these high boots. (Courtesy of Acadia National Park.)

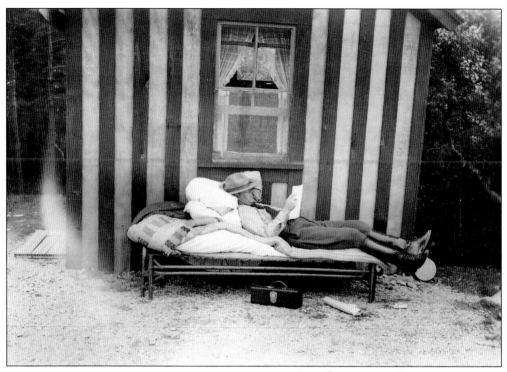

In order to ensure their presentations were apt and accurate, rangers prepared lectures. Here, John Pierce lies on a cot outside his cabin while reading material for his presentation. A July 1933 handout of ranger-led programs lists short nature walks for children, an afternoon nature walk for YWCA girls and Girl Scouts, and mountain climbing for Boy Scouts and boys of that age. (Courtesy of Acadia National Park.)

In this photograph entitled "Richard Manville Lecturing," Manville explains to park visitors how at about one to two hours before high tide, particularly if there is wind, the sound of a receding wave resembles the sound of thunder, hence the name Thunder Hole. The surf has sometimes sprayed as high as 40 feet (or 12 meters) upon hitting Thunder Hole. (Courtesy of Acadia National Park.)

Today, the stone stairs leading down from Ocean Drive to a viewing platform have sturdy railings and gates to close sections of the walkway if the surf is too high, but there was little protection in place in the 1930s. (Right, courtesy of Maine Historic Preservation Commission; below, courtesy of Acadia National Park.)

These people are scattered all over the rocks near Thunder Hole and not necessarily wearing shoes that will keep them from slipping on wet rocks. In recent years, people have been swept into the ocean. Like Thunder Hole, Otter Cliffs also has spectacularly high surf. Today, this many people would probably not be standing on the rocks watching the surf with rangers present. But watching the surf remains a long-standing tradition, particularly if storm conditions combine to produce dramatic surf. (Courtesy of Acadia National Park.)

National Park Service director Arno Cammerer (seated behind the ranger) enjoyed a naturalist sea cruise on one of his visits to Acadia; following the cruise, Cammerer thanks the captain as he leaves the yacht *Narmada*. Cammerer initially worked as the assistant director to Stephen Mather and was considered his right-hand man in Washington. In August 1933, he succeeded Horace Albright to become the third director. During his tenure, parklands tripled, public facilities were improved, and visitation jumped from 2 million to 16 million persons. Under his watch, Congress passed legislation establishing the Historic Sites Act. In Acadia, Cammerer supported building the Cadillac Mountain Road so that people who could not climb could also reach the summit and admire the views. Cammerer's biography on a National Park Service site notes that "his contributions to the National Park Service were legion." (Both, courtesy of Acadia National Park.)

The young lady seems disengaged in the above photograph but more attentive in the image below. Barnacles cover the rocks the people are standing on and the rocks behind them. One of the first animals encountered in a tide pool or around rocky areas at low tide are barnacles. When the tide comes in and covers them, they feed using their six pairs of feathery legs to gather and eat plankton. Often mussels are covered with barnacles. They, too, eat plankton but filter their food from the water. Most tide pools have periwinkles and snails, which are edible and quite delicious, and some tide pools have sea stars. The park continues to offer naturalist tours of tide pools, and they often book early. (Both, courtesy of Acadia National Park.)

Today, people wearing dress shoes are discouraged from walking on the rocks since they are very slippery. This appears not to be of concern to early visitors to Acadia. Maurice Sullivan talks about tide pools to a group on Burnt Porcupine, one of the four Porcupine Islands in Frenchman Bay. The larger-shaped shells are probably mussels; these are also edible, and people gather them outside the park. (Courtesy of Acadia National Park.)

On one of the nature tours that ranger-naturalist Maurice Sullivan led in the late 1930s, a woman plays an accordion while most passengers sing. The *Bar Harbor Times* in its 75th anniversary supplement on Acadia notes that Sullivan led many boat trips, some to the outer islands. That piece, "Remembering," also quotes him as saying he remembers overnights on Cadillac and singing under the stars. (Courtesy of Acadia National Park.)

The ranger at the far end of the group on the lower ledge explains that the Precipice Trail, designed by Rudolph Brunnow of the Bar Harbor VIA, requires hikers to use ladders and rungs to access the summit. Since 1989, the trail has regularly closed in spring to protect the nesting efforts of peregrine falcons. It reopens once the chicks fledge. (Courtesy of Bar Harbor Historical Society collection.)

This overlook is above what is now the Bear Brook Picnic Area, but in the early years of the park, the area was a campground. In the far distance is Robin Hood Park. Owned by Edward Morrell of Philadelphia, Robin Hood Park was the site of a three-day horse show held annually near the end of August from 1900 to 1912. (Courtesy of Acadia National Park.)

When Bar Harbor native Benjamin Hadley retired from the military as a commander, he applied for a position at Acadia. Eventually he became George Dorr's assistant superintendent and on Dorr's death was promoted to superintendent. He brought to his position both an understanding of Bar Harbor politics and strong administrative skills. Following Dorr's death, Hadley played a critical role in advocating for the Dorr Memorial at Sieur de Monts Spring. (Courtesy of Acadia National Park.)

Beginning in 1930, Arda Tarbell (right), a 25-year-old from Aroostook County, became Acadia's chief clerk and administrative officer. She shepherded the park through acquiring lands and surviving the Great Depression, World War II, and the 1947 wildfire. In addition to her administrative work, she also developed an oral history. Here she is with Sylvia Young Cough (left), the assistant secretary to the superintendent working under Tarbell. (Courtesy of Acadia National Park.)

Pictured here is Acadia's staff in front of headquarters on Park Street. With the designation of the Sieur de Monts National Monument in 1916, George Dorr, its first superintendent with an annual salary of $12, paid for the construction of this building. After the new headquarters in Hulls Cove opened, this building was moved to College of the Atlantic as part of the Dorr Museum of Natural History. From left to right are (first row) Grace Oaks; Audra Tarbell, chief clerk; Joe Conroy; Carl Novak, chief clerk; Benjamin Hadley, superintendent; George Dorr, first superintendent; Kathleen Stevens, superintendent's secretary; and Natalie Appleby; (second row) Ralph Douglas, chief of maintenance; Ben Breeze, landscape architect; Maurice Sullivan, naturalist; William Campbell, motor cycle patrol; Orient Thompson, ranger; Dick Sherman; Serenus Rodick, liaison attorney between the National Park Service and John D. Rockefeller Jr.; and Dana Young, Dorr's chauffeur. (Courtesy of Acadia National Park.)

Six

EXPERIENCING ACADIA

Built by the Town of Bar Harbor in the 1890s, Ocean Drive provided access to those who simply wanted to watch the ocean and the tides or to enjoy a picnic. Rocks such as these were also favored by young people who jumped from rock to rock and found tide pools to explore. (Courtesy of Maine Historic Preservation Commission.)

While it is not clear where Margaret Lawrence (who cannot be further identified) is cooking, it could be breakfast on Cadillac. For some years, the park provided wood and cooking areas for those coming to see the sunrise. There is some dispute as to whether Cadillac or Eastport, Maine, which is farther down the coast, is the first place on the East Coast to see the sunrise. (Courtesy of Acadia National Park.)

What better way to end a picnic in Acadia than to toast marshmallows along the shore, either over the fire in one of the park's picnic areas, at a campsite in Acadia, or at one of the many private campsites on Mount Desert Island and in the Winter Harbor/Schoodic area. (Courtesy of Acadia National Park.)

Going by boat to an island for a picnic or overnight is a long-standing tradition for year-round and summer residents. Arriving on one of these offshore islands requires motoring out in a larger boat and then getting into a dingy that ferries passengers to shore. Named for the ash-colored rocks on its southeastern shore, Burnt Porcupine is the only one of the four Porcupine Islands not owned by Acadia. (Courtesy of Acadia National Park.)

To ensure visitors disembark safely, there is a person on shore who keeps the dingy near the wooden plank so that no one has to step into the water. Today, people dress more casually for picnics and wear shoes appropriate for walking on the rocky beach—a beach that is typical of the shoreline on islands in Frenchman Bay. (Courtesy of Acadia National Park.)

Like other offshore islands, Burnt Porcupine is a favorite of many birders. With her binoculars, this woman has come prepared to add to her list of birds. The four Porcupines derive their name from their shape. In addition to Burnt Porcupine, there are three others: Long Porcupine, the largest; Bald Porcupine, with high barren cliffs; and Sheep Porcupine, where sheep grazed. (Courtesy of Acadia National Park.)

As this 1937 photograph shows, once ashore, visitors, in addition to picnicking and birding, explore tide pools and share what they find. Typically, one finds these pools among the ledges where ocean water is trapped as the tide goes out. In these pools at low tide, one finds barnacles, whelks, limpets, and seaweed. (Courtesy of Acadia National Park.)

Once Mount Desert Island became a flourishing summer colony, many summer people owned boats that they sailed with friends. "Cottages," as these large, spacious homes were called, dot the hillside, while a number of sailboats float on moorings in the harbor. (Courtesy of Acadia National Park.)

Often when young people are sailing or as in this case on a motor yacht, they are asked if they want to take the wheel, and generally they do. This "Young Skipper at the Helm" is on the yacht *Narmada*. Taking the wheel introduces aspiring skippers to the effect of wind on the direction and stability of the boat—something that is particularly important when sailing. (Courtesy of Acadia National Park.)

Years ago, people sailed to move people and goods from place to place or to fish or for whaling. Capt. Grafton W. Pinkham takes this group out on a pleasure sail. Towing a dinghy indicates they probably plan to sail to an offshore island or a beach with no dock. It is not uncommon today to have an experienced sailor—and his outfit suggests he is—captain the boat. (Courtesy of Acadia National Park.)

The *Appalachian Mountain Club Guide* recommends climbing both Penobscot and Sargent Mountains, whose summits are about a mile apart. Nestled between the two mountains lies Sargent Pond, where climbers can take a refreshing swim. A .3-mile trail connecting the two summits skirts the south shore and provides easy access to the pond. (Courtesy of Acadia National Park.)

During the last ice age, Mount Desert Island was covered with glaciers. As glaciers retreated, cirques, or bowl-shaped depressions, formed with some becoming ponds. In Acadia there are two cirques—the Bowl between the Beehive and Gorham Mountain and Sargent Pond (pictured here). Plant pollen cores from the bottom of this pond suggest this is the first lake that formed in what became Maine. Penobscot Mountain rises in the background. (Courtesy of Acadia National Park.)

A long-standing pastime in Acadia is walking along the many paths and carriage roads. Mrs. Price is joined on this path by Clio Chilcott and Nancy Blackwell of New York visiting Miss Silsby in Ellsworth, all attired in their walking clothes. Chilcott lectured on Lafayette National Park—an earlier name of Acadia. (Courtesy of Acadia National Park.)

John D. Rockefeller Jr. built and, until his death in 1960, maintained 57 miles of carriage roads—some on his property and some on parkland. Initially, these roads were primarily for carriages and walkers, and they gradually became popular with bikers and with cross-country skiers and snowmobilers in winter. From this road paralleling the west side of Jordan Pond, park visitors can access carriage roads around Eagle Lake and Duck Brook. (Courtesy of Library of Congress.)

Since the late 1800s, those hiking the Acadia Mountain Trail have spectacular views of Somes Sound and Norumbega Mountain on the east side of Somes Sound. This trail was originally laid out by the Southwest Harbor Village Improvement Society and is now maintained by the park. (Courtesy of Acadia National Park.)

These horseback riders are riding along the north shore of Eagle Lake. While horseback riding is allowed on many of the carriage roads, it is now prohibited from this section of the Eagle Lake Loop. In the distance rise the North and South Bubbles. (Courtesy of Acadia National Park.)

While many visiting Acadia National Park since the 1980s think rock climbing is a relatively new sport, in the 1930s, many people climbed. It is just that the gear was different. The climbers in the above photograph appear to be assessing their climb up the South Bubble. Climbing the South Bubble in the late 1930s meant climbers were all roped together, not with a hook on a harness but with the rope itself tied around the waist of each climber. (Both, courtesy of Acadia National Park.)

In the above image, the gentleman is belaying the rope; the belayer's job is to take up slack or let out the rope. Here, the rope looks fairly taut. In the photograph below, the woman is slowly but steadily moving up the face of the cliff on the South Bubble, a climbing area still popular today. (Both, courtesy of Acadia National Park.)

Driving the Ocean Drive section of the Loop Road provides many opportunities to get out and walk along the Ocean Path or the trail around Otter Point. While some park in what is now the Gorham Mountain parking lot—a lot across from Otter Point—others elect to park along the roadside. Acadia National Park's digital photographs and archives have many references to auto caravans. On some occasions, a ranger meets the caravan to explain the significance of a particular site such as Thunder Hole or Otter Cliffs. (Both, courtesy of Acadia National Park.)

Sargent Drive is a narrow 3.5-mile road along the east side of Somes Sound. Formed by retreating glaciers over 18,000 years ago, Somes Sound divides Mount Desert Island into two sections. While it has some characteristics of fiords, today geologists say it is not a true fiord and refer to it as being fiord like. Looking across the sound to the west, these visitors see the village of Hall Quarry; Acadia and St. Sauveur Mountains; and Valley Cove, where Man O' War Brook flows into the sound. The *Appalachian Mountain Club Guide* notes that, because of the deep water there, frigates often anchored and replenished water supplies. (Both, courtesy of Acadia National Park.)

According to Acadia National Park's archival notes, in July 1937 a group that included Mrs. McElroy and Col. William Jay Schieffelin, neither of whom is further identified, went out fishing off Great Duck Island, a 220-acre island 10 miles due south of Northeast Harbor. While many residents and visitors try their luck at fishing, not all are as lucky as Mrs. McElroy and Colonel Schieffelin, both of whom caught good-sized cod. Since the early 17th century, cod, which can be salted, was a mainstay of the economy along the Eastern Seaboard of the United States and Maritime Canada. (Both, courtesy of Acadia National Park.)

After a heavy snowfall, George Dorr (right) and another person, in the archives identified as "possibly Benjamin Hadley," snowshoe near the banks of Duck Brook. Snowshoeing on the paths and carriage roads, a long-standing tradition in Acadia, allows residents and visitors to experience the quietness of the woods and catch glimpses of resident birds. (Courtesy of Acadia National Park.)

In the 1930s and again in the late 1960s, there were rope tows on McFarland Hill, a mountain with a 200-foot vertical drop located just across from park headquarters on Route 233. The first rope tow, founded in 1936 by the Mount Desert Outing Club, burned in the 1947 wildfire. Subsequently, as local historian Don Lenehan notes, Aldene Robbins and Roy McFarland purchased the mountain in the 1960s from the Mount Desert Outing Club and Roy's father. These two photographs, taken in the 1960s, show the rope tow in operation. (Both, courtesy of Acadia National Park.)

A Bar Harbor Historical Society online exhibit includes a number of comments from those who skied down McFarland Hill in the 1960s—comments that talk about the two warming huts, one at the bottom and another at the summit. These comments also mention several trails. As these people ski down, they have views of snow-covered Cadillac Mountain. (Courtesy of Acadia National Park.)

One way to get exercise in winter and to enjoy the outdoors is to cross-country ski, and if one is the first to break trail, that person will truly get an extensive workout. Today, thanks to an endowment in memory of Lelia Bright, cross-country trails on many of the 57 miles of carriage roads are groomed by volunteers. (Both, courtesy of Acadia National Park.)

As the smiles on these young people's faces indicate, tobogganing is fun. While the Acadia National Park archives do not indicate where they are tobogganing, it could be Kebo Valley Golf Club, where many still sled in winter. (Courtesy of Acadia National Park.)

While the archival notes refer to this as a child's stroller, with its runners it appears to be more of a sled. It is unlike many of today's children's sleds that are pulled rather than pushed, and obviously the seat is wide enough not just for the child but the dog as well—perfect for skating on Eagle Lake. Written in pencil under the photograph is "Mrs. Dick Wasgath." (Courtesy of Acadia National Park.)

This quintessential postcard shows people of all ages in a range of winter activities. Some skate, others skate sail, and still others appear to be in carriages, but how these are propelled is not clear. (Courtesy of Jesup Memorial Library.)

Once the ice on Eagle Lake is hard enough, young people—and sometimes adults—start a pickup game of hockey. While initially the game may only be between two, others join in once they arrive at the lake. The mountain to the left is Cadillac; the Bubbles are at the far end of the lake. (Courtesy of Stephen Ressel.)

While some play hockey, others simply skate sail or skate around Eagle Lake, the largest lake on the east side of Mount Desert Island. Although there are no ice fishing huts in this photograph, ice fishing is another popular activity when the ice is strong enough to hold both the hut and the truck that people use to access their hut. (Courtesy of Stephen Ressel.)

In the early 1900s, skate sailing was introduced in North America. To skate sail, Frank Gray, who skate sailed on Eagle Lake in the late 1930s, put the sail, which resembles a kite, on his right shoulder so that the wind could blow him down the ice as he skated. To reverse direction, he moved the sail to his left shoulder. The archival notes say, "Frank Gray skate sailing." (Courtesy of Acadia National Park.)

As these two photographs taken in the 1930s show, some enjoy skate sailing as part of a group while others are happy to meld with other skaters. Eagle Lake, which is located off Route 233 and has a boat landing, makes a perfect place in winter to launch skate sails and in summer canoes and motorboats. Before modern refrigeration, ice was regularly harvested from Eagle Lake and stored for use in the summer. (Both, courtesy of Acadia National Park.)

Experiencing Acadia National Park would not have been possible without the vision and commitment of George Dorr and Stephen Mather, an industrialist, conservationist, and first director of the National Park Service. A plaque on the summit of Cadillac credits Mather with laying the "foundation of the National Park Service defining and establishing the policies under which its areas shall be developed and conserved unimpaired for future generations. There will never come an end to the good that he has done." Mather visited Acadia several times and, along with Dorr and John D. Rockefeller Jr., stressed developing the infrastructure to ensure access for all. Dorr's plaque at Sieur de Monts Spring calls him a "gentleman scholar, lover of nature, father of this national park steadfast in his zeal to make the beauty of this island available to all." (Courtesy of Acadia National Park.)

Bibliography

"Acadia National Park at 100: A Centennial Celebration." *Mount Desert Islander*, 2016.

"Acadia National Park Celebrates 75 Years." *Bar Harbor Times*, 1991.

Brechlin, Earl. "Third Generation Continues Carriage Road Legacy." *Acadia: The Friends of Acadia Journal*, Summer 2021: 10–12.

Brown, Margaret Coffin. *Pathmakers: Cultural Landscape Report for the Historic Hiking Trail System Mount Desert Island*. Boston, MA: Olmsted Center for Landscape Preservation, National Park Service, 2006.

Dorr, George B. *The Story of Acadia National Park*. 2nd edition. Bar Harbor, ME: Acadia Publishing, 1985.

Epp, Ronald H. *Creating Acadia National Park: The Biography of George Bucknam Dorr*. Bar Harbor, ME: Friends of Acadia, 2016.

Grossman, Leo. *Cadillac Mountain Highway Project Diary* and Leo Grossman Papers, 1927–1944. Historical Archival Collection, Acadia National Park.

Killon, Jeffrey, and H. Eliot Foulds. *Cultural Landscape Report for the Historic Motor Road System, Acadia National Park*. Boston, MA: Olmsted Center for Landscape Preservation, National Park Service, 2006.

Lenahan, Donald P. *The Memorials of Acadia National Park*. Bar Harbor, ME: D.P. Lenahan, 2010.

Maher, Neil. "Route 233 Bridge (Eagle Lake Road Overpass)." Historic American Engineering Record, No. ME-17, 1995.

Quin, Richard H. "Cadillac Mountain Road." Historic American Engineering Record, No. ME-58, 1994.

———. "Eagle Lake Road Bridge: Spanning Carriage Road on Eagle Lake Road." Historic American Engineering Record, ME-55, 1996.

———. "Spanning Duck Brook between Witch Hole Loop Road and New Eagle Lake (Motor Road)." Historic American Engineering Record, ME-40. 1994.

———. "Spanning Duck Brook on the Paradise Hill Road." Historic American Engineering Record, ME-30, 1994.

———. "Spanning New Eagle Lake Road on Paradise Hill Road." Historic American Engineering Record, ME-18, 1996.

———. "Spanning Stanley Brook, Stanley Brook Motor Road, and Seaside Trail on Barr Hill, Day Mountain Carriage Road." Historic American Engineering Record, ME-45, 1994.

DISCOVER THOUSANDS OF LOCAL HISTORY BOOKS FEATURING MILLIONS OF VINTAGE IMAGES

Arcadia Publishing, the leading local history publisher in the United States, is committed to making history accessible and meaningful through publishing books that celebrate and preserve the heritage of America's people and places.

Find more books like this at
www.arcadiapublishing.com

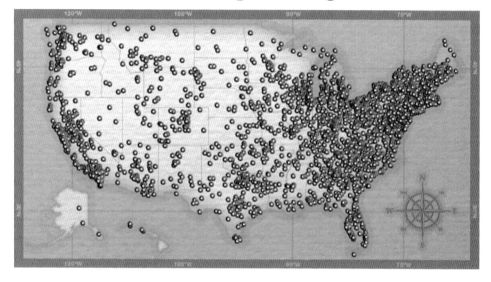

Search for your hometown history, your old stomping grounds, and even your favorite sports team.